Beautiful
Las Vegas
and
Southern Nevada

"Learn about America in a beautiful way."

Beautiful
Las Vegas
and
Southern Nevada

Concept and Design: Robert D. Shangle
Text: Duke London

First Printing September, 1980
Published by Beautiful America Publishing Company
P.O. Box 608, Beaverton, Oregon 97075
Robert D. Shangle, Publisher

Library of Congress Cataloging in Publication Data
Beautiful Las Vegas and Southern Nevada
1. Las Vegas, Nev.—Description—Views. I. London, Duke.
F849.L35B37   979.3'13   79-18837
ISBN 0-89802-079-4
ISBN 0-89802-078-6 (paperback)

Contents

Enlarged Prints

Most of the photography in this book is available as photographic
enlargements. Send self-addressed, stamped envelope for information.
For a complete product catalog, send $1.00.
Beautiful America Publishing Company
P.O. Box 608
Beaverton, Oregon 97075

Introduction

Las Vegas is one of a relatively few American places with names likely to be recognized anywhere in the world. Exactly why that is true would be hard to say: Las Vegas finds itself in the company of world-stature cities like New York and San Francisco in that regard, but also with Disneyland. Fame, pure and simple, is the only common denominator; they all have made names for themselves, and they are instantly identifiable by almost anyone in the world as American places. *Everybody* has heard about Las Vegas.

Exactly *what* everybody has heard is not so easy to ascertain: Las Vegas is a favorite subject for commentators who want to make a point, and it has probably been called everything, at least once. ''Glitter City,'' some folks name it. Las Vegas rises from the desert like some huge exotic plant that takes its nutrition from the air, the way an orchid does, not depending upon the land for support. ''Sin City,'' others have called it, though they would probably have to admit that the sins they have in mind were not invented in Las Vegas, nor practiced there exclusively. ''Fun City'' is what the Chamber of Commerce calls it, with some justification; but you'll notice right away that they don't call themselves the ''Chamber of Fun.'' In Las Vegas, fun *is* business. The descriptions roll on and on: Vegas belongs to everybody, it seems, and everybody has something to say about it. Meanwhile, with the brash, sometimes naive vitality of a natural winner, Las Vegas goes on doing what it does best: playing, making money, and getting famous.

Critics of the Las Vegas ''scene,'' in the long run, end up talking more about themselves than about Las Vegas. The guy from New Jersey tells you more than you ever wanted to know about his life and hard times as a gambler; the writer from the frozen midwest demonstrates that he was looking for something sleazy—and found it. A novelist from the coast sees the town mostly in the context of the crumbling marriage he is there to get out of. And someone dolorously intones from the far side of the continent that if it weren't for gambling, there would be no reason for the city of Las Vegas to exist at all. The only faction that usually isn't heard from is the folks who live there.

The fact sometimes gets lost in the hype, but there are about 300,000 people who call Las Vegas home. People live there; they get up in the morning and go to work, get the kids off to school, plan weekends at the lake or in the mountains. Artists create, college students study, ministers preach, ranchers ride their fencelines, just like people anywhere. A great many folks *do* work in the entertainment industry—it's the mainstay of the local economy. But they're like people anywhere else when it comes to blowing a chunk of the family income for a night on the town: it's a special occasion, not a regular event. The ''natives'' of Las Vegas are a lot like the Nevadan who told me: ''All I know for sure about gambling is that it paid 80 percent of the state's taxes last year.''

It is easy to get the impression that there are two Las Vegases, a pair of cities that operate under the same name, in the same place. The city of the visitor, the media, the nightlife and the high-rollers is one side of Las Vegas, full of people who fly in for a few days to have some fun and go a round or two with Lady Luck. And then there is the day life, the life of the folks who live there, in a desert culture that in spite of everything manages to hang on to a little of its Old West background.

The city of the visitor is the legendary Las Vegas. Its population is about 35,000—approximately the same as the number of hotel and motel rooms in town. They come, of course, for the gambling, which is headquartered in downtown's Casino Center and the posh motels of The Strip. The action goes on around the clock, with a variety and color that beggar description: these are people, after all, who have come from considerable distance for the sole purpose of having a good time. Las Vegas tries hard not to disappoint.

There are two classic views of this Las Vegas. One is the sight of town as you approach from the desert at night, when the neon extravaganzas of Casino Center and the Strip brighten the sky and blaze for miles across the valley floor. Some folks think that this is the best view of all. They are the kind of people who like to back off a ways and take it all in, full of light and motion but slightly dissociated from the reality of cityness, a great heap of light on the landscape. The other favorite view is downtown's Casino Center, called Glitter Gulch for reasons that are good and sufficient. In Glitter Gulch the abstraction is gone: the lighting is hard, immediate, boisterous, exuberant . . . the same as the crowds around you. Either view will compel you to concede that, forgetting good taste for a moment, neon has never been put to more creative and extravagant use than in Las Vegas. There may not be such a thing as tasteful neon anyway.

Over on the Strip, the lights spell out one of the benefits of having all that money in town: Entertainment, with a capital E. Big names, extravagant floor shows and incredible spectacle are part of the everyday here. It's always Saturday night in Las Vegas, and sometimes, from the look of the marquees, you would be inclined to guess that there was no one left to hold the fort in Hollywood. The Chamber of Commerce—or Chamber of Fun, if you'd rather—lists some 25 clubs which routinely feature international celebrities in their presentations; and of lesser-known entertainments there is no end.

What is useful to keep in mind about the visitors' Las Vegas, that strange, half-city, half-dreamland in the desert, is that it is a business. Gambling, in particular, is big business, and the first rule of successful businesses is that they take in more money than they give out. That is probably all you need to know about gambling. The rest, of course, is window-dressing, something to attract and entertain the guests who play at the slots or the tables; and no matter what the bewildering and phantasmagorice array of diversion, it all runs at a profit.

But there is that other Las Vegas: a city of 300,000 people who live there year-around, enjoying the desert climate, the natural and recreational resources of Southern Nevada, and the dynamic atmosphere of this improbable boomtown. They call it home, and in a great many ways, some of the nicest things about Las Vegas belong to the people who live there. They are the ones who may, occasionally, watch the sun rise over barren and grand expanses of lonely desert. They will get the year-around enjoyment of Lake Mead, that striking juxtaposition of desert and water; they will savor the sight of thunderstorms over the mountains; and striding through ghost towns or mining camps, they will perhaps feel admiration for an earlier breed of men who fought for survival against the very desert that people now flock to enjoy.

Like many American cities, Las Vegas has grown beyond the relationship with the land that was its first reason for being. Once it was simply an oasis, offering the gift of water in the parched desert, a stopping place on the way through instead of a destination in itself. It became a target for settlement by missionaries who hoped to civilize local Indians: of that encounter neither Indians nor missionaries remain—only the desert. There followed a hardy race of men who were able to take from the desert what it had to offer; to take the rudiments of a living from a land that didn't part with them easily. No matter how you look at it, it's still desert. This land will support grazing to a certain extent. It can water only a limited number of fields. There may, as prospectors claim, still be gold, silver, uranium and copper in those hills, but not in unlimited quantity; and getting it out is hard work. If Las Vegas was forced to live off the land, it would be a much smaller town than it is today.

The cowboy, the sheepherder, the prospector, and the farmer all have cherished places in the history—and the present-day life—of the Las Vegas area. On the level that the desert will support, those activities still go on, and they impart a flavor to the region that no amount of glitter can erase. But to raise Las Vegas from its dependence on the land took some of the tricks of the 20th century: the technology to deal with the desert, and the ability to make your limitations work in your favor. Even the harsh and demanding desert can be a valuable natural resource if you have the means of selling it to—for instance—farmers in Minnesota, where the mercury disappears into the bottom of the thermometer for months at a time. Las Vegas is a child of the 20th century. When businessmen figured out how to sell the sunshine, enlivened by a little gambling and some entertainment, the town embarked on a boom that hasn't stopped. Two-thirds of all the buildings in Las Vegas are less than 20 years old; most of the residents of the city are from somewhere else originally. Still, it's a western town, a desert town, a place where outdoor recreation is plentiful and close at hand, a place where you can support a family. The people who live there like it.

There is a lot to be said for both Las Vegases. There is a lot that has been said about Glitter City, pro and con. Everybody needs a night on the town once in a while, and if it's true that you can get anything you want in Las Vegas, it is also true that you don't have to take anything you don't want. Here is a challenge for you. Have your night on the town. Enjoy. then spend a *day* on the town—and on the desert. Meander on the campus, visit some of the art galleries, get on out to Lake Mead and play in the water. Drop into a ghost town and scare up some ghosts; drive up to Mt. Charleston and let the big view sink in.

That way you'll find out what everybody knows about Las Vegas, and more: the glitter and the grit, the International Phenomenon and the down-home side of this world-stature city.

Duke London

A Short History

You don't have to go far from that strange, night-blooming flower, which is Las Vegas, before you find yourself in a different, almost timeless world. Away from the glitter and gold of the Strip, out where the brightest light by day is the sun, by night, the moon and stars, the ''other world'' of Southern Nevada waits for folks who care to find it. The ''payoffs'' of this world, for those lucky enough to know it, might be flapjacks over a morning campfire, a cool drink from a bubbling mountain spring, or lungs full of crystal clear air.

This is country big enough for a person to throw back his shoulders and holler—and have his echo as the only answer. It is desert and mountain land, with the Virgin River and the great Colorado cutting through in circular sweeps. Nature gave this region mountain aspen trees in groves that shed a yellow carpet during Indian summer; sun that bakes the earth and turns sagebrush brown; cactus and bright blooming plants that make the high desert a greenhouse of glory after infrequent rains. The tortured landscape looks as if the earth has been torn apart and pushed back together. That is just about how it happened. The mountain ranges running north and south are remnants of the places where giant slabs met. Geologists say that the earth in this region sank below the sea many times, eventually rising to become the high desert that leads to the Rocky Mountains. Earthquakes and volcanos were common in the far-removed past and the ground burned and then froze, cracked and lifted. It is no wonder that the area became one of contrasts.

The desert is the lowest common denominator of man and animal. It weeds out the best and keeps them; only the tough survive. Coyotes, roadrunners, burros, rabbits, kangaroo rats, lizards, and snakes thrive here, as do Joshua trees, yucca, creosote bush, mesquite and different varieties of cactus. The plants for the most part turn a hostile face to the elements with spines and needles. There is a solitude, a stark intensity to the desert. The heat and wind, the dust and vastness of it all can make a soul feel completely alone. As the sun sets in a shower of red and yellow, it is impossible to conceive how this land once was. Prehistoric man hunted mammoths

9

and ground sloth in a climate that was humid: the desert at one time has seen elephants and jungle.

In 1933, an area located ten miles north of Las Vegas, Tule Springs, was staked out by archaeologists. They uncovered bones of extinct camels, horses, and a bison with a flint projectile still embedded in it. From the bones, scientists were able to determine that animals had inhabited the rain forests 28,000 years ago. A four-and-a-half month dig yielded two-hundred-thousand tons of dirt, and enough evidence to support the theory that man had dwelled in the Las Vegas area 12,000 years ago.

Those first-known inhabitants of the Las Vegas area were the Anasazi Indian tribe. They were nomads and gatherers, hunting antelope, deer and mountain sheep, living in pit houses roofed with mesquite and sagebrush. Eventually, they discovered the comforts of a more stable life, dwelling in adobe house clusters, blocking off river water for irrigation, raising squash, beans, corn and sunflowers. The know-how they developed in raising cotton has particularly interested archaeologists. Then, apparently during a time of war between Indian nations, the Anasazi gave up their ''civilization'' and moved for a time to the nearly-inaccessible cliffs that overlook the Las Vegas valley. Finally . . . they disappeared. It is one of the world's archaeological mysteries.

A great deal of time passed before other people inhabited the area, and these were the blood stock of the Southern Paiute nation. To the Paiutes, life was a matter of living one day at a time. They made homes from bullrushes, skinned animals for clothing, and ate when they found food. Into this routine came the fur trappers, men like the famous Jedediah Smith, who in 1826 followed the course of the Colorado River. After him came the explorer, Captain John C. Fremont.

In 1844, Fremont made this note in his diary: ''. . . a camping ground this day called Las Vegas . . . . Two narrow streams of water, four or five feet deep, gush suddenly, with a quick current, from two large springs . . . the taste of the water is good but rather too warm to be agreeable.''

The first settling of the valley came with William Bringhurst and 30 other men sent by Brigham Young, who told them, ''Go to Las Vegas, build a fort there to protect the immigrants, and teach the Indians.'' Bringhurst was named president of the mission on January 10, 1856. But within a few years the mission was abandoned, and though the building stayed, the Mormons did not. Indians harvested the fields that had been planted, and eventually the mission grounds returned to mesquite and the dams and bridges floated away.

The next occupant of Las Vegas was the U.S. Army, who held the territory during the Civil War to protect the southern route to California. In 1882, the water rights were acquired by Archibald Stewart, an original '49er. Stewart's wife accompanied him to Las Vegas with their two children, and while they lived there three more children were born. Archibald was killed, suddenly, in a quarrel with a neighboring rancher. When Mrs. Stewart heard the news, she immediately set off on horseback and brought her husband home. But at home there was no lumber, so Mrs. Stewart removed the doors from the hinges and used them to build a coffin.

In 1902, the San Pedro, Los Angeles and Salt Lake Railroad bought the ranchsite at "The Meadows," and in 1905, city lots were sold at auction. The railroad's announcement that Las Vegas would be a major division point on the route, which would stretch from the Atlantic to the Pacific, revived the American belief in the frontier. When the auctioneer began his cry, there was nothing but the idea of building a town. Two days later, when he yelled "Sold!" and brought down his gavel for the final time, 1,200 lots had changed hands.

In 1940, Las Vegas was described as ". . . a bit of roulette in the evenings; health-seekers basking in the brilliant sunshine; an occasional Paiute woman with a baby cradled on her back; toothless old prospectors in town for a new grubstake; cowboys rolling along in elaborate high-heeled boots; ranchers and their wives buying supplies and seeing the latest movies; young people rushing down to Lake Mead to swim or up to camp or ski in the Charleston Mountains; men and women of any age on their way to the stables for horses, local men and women going to rehearsals of little theater groups."

That was before Las Vegas became the glitter city.

A City To Live In

The astonishing growth of Las Vegas in its first 50 years, no matter how amazing it seems, is pale in comparison to the activity of the last two decades. The town has doubled in size every ten years to the current population of more than 300,000. And just as noticeable has been the change in the atmosphere of Las Vegas from the rural community to a "city of the world." The old west is still in Las Vegas, but these days it is hidden behind the bright lights of a brand new city: an "old" building in this town is one that has been standing more than 20 years.

The railroad and agriculture were the primary developers at first, but in 1931, gambling was legalized, providing the real impetus for the Las Vegas boom. Since World War II there has been nothing with which to compare the "Entertainment Capital of the World." The super stars of show business regularly play the Strip and Casino Center showplaces, which have names familiar to nearly every American: Caesar's Palace, Aladdin, Circus Circus, Desert Inn, Dunes, Flamingo Hilton, MGM Grand, Mint, Sahara, The Sands . . . .

The folks who live in Las Vegas know all that: for many of them, the entertainment industry is, in some sense, the source of the weekly paycheck. (However, a glance at the Las Vegas telephone directory's Yellow Pages might convince you that air-conditioning technologists outnumber all other occupational groups in town.) The point is, however, that the things that make Las Vegas a fun place to visit don't necessarily make it a nice place to live, and vice-versa. Visitors frequently don't stray from Glitter City to find out what sort of attractions appeal to the folks who make Las Vegas their home. That, according to home folks, makes visitors the losers.

The pride of Las Vegas is the University of Nevada, Las Vegas. The university has emerged as a proud standard of progress, uniting the school and the community it serves. On campus a visitor can view pre-historic Indian artifacts, live reptiles, and natural history displays at the UNLV Museum of Natural History. Science Hall houses one of the largest mineral collections to be found in Nevada. If an evening is to be spent with culture, Artemus W. Ham Concert Hall is a good bet, with performances throughout the year with some of the world's finest symphony orchestras, opera companies, jazz ensembles, ballet troupes, and folk and pop music artists.

Like everything else in Las Vegas, the campus of UNLV is brand, spanking new. The first college-level classes did not begin in Southern Nevada until Dr. James Dickinson, in 1951, offered an extension course in a spare room at Las Vegas High School. Six years later the university was founded by action of the Nevada Board of Regents. In the summer of 1957, the University, located on 60 acres of desert land, opened its doors to a pioneer class of 300. Bachelor degrees were awarded for the first time in 1964, when 29 students qualified for graduation.

Today, with a faculty of more than 300 full-time professors, UNLV has more instructors than there were students in 1957. The student population now stands at more than 9,000. With the addition of faculty and students from every section of the United States, and also several foreign countries, the campus, as well as the community, has acquired something of an international flavor. The average student is young, about 25 years of age. As testimony to the industriousness of these students, three out of four of them work at full or part-time jobs in addition to attending classes.

Education, although important to any city, is but a spoke in the wheel. Rounding out the other aspects of Las Vegas are 150 churches, a statistic which ranks Las Vegas high in the nation on a church-per-capita basis. Three daily newspapers, the *Las Vegas Sun*, *Review Journal* and *Valley Times*, serve the greater Las Vegas area. There are eleven radio stations, five television stations and three fine libraries: Las Vegas Public Library, Clark County Library, and the library at the University.

If the Old West is hard to find anymore in the cosmopolitan atmosphere of Las Vegas, it is alive and well in the arts. The late painter Buster Wilson saw the region through the eyes of a native. A Paiute Indian, he spent his life in the desert and among the forested trails of his Spring Mountain Ranch. From an early age he sketched the beauty of the cactus and blooming desert flowers, painting what he saw around him. It might have been a solitary bald eagle soaring in white, puffy clouds above a canyon, or an old Indian woman alone on the broad expanse of the desert. He was a friend to all the wild creatures. In one of his last poems he wrote: ''I will always feel the whisper of the desert wind, smell the sage, and see the stars above the mountaintops.'' Buster Wilson is gone, but the land, which lent inspiration to him, has had the same effect on others.

Since Buster Wilson, a number of artists have discovered the world of pre-civilization, enriching the Las Vegas area with more than a dozen quality galleries. For a newcomer, it takes time to find the beauty and expression of the desert. While most climates are brilliant green in spring and summer, the desert, with its subtleties, is a totally different environment. Color is quieter in the desert, and an artist must listen harder: the soft, delicate quality of the desert, when observed in perspective, is more impressive than a flood of brilliant hues. Newcomer and old-timer alike provide Las Vegas gallery-goers with an unparalleled opportunity to witness desert drama, and scenes from the passing of the Old West.

Outside Of Town

About 25,000 visitors a day enjoy the sunshine, the entertainment, and the chance to participate in legal gambling in the city of Las Vegas. The tourists, who venture away from downtown, are searching for either desert or water, and this region has an abundance of both.

The water is Lake Mead, made by a 110-mile long reservoir that developed when Hoover Dam was built across the mighty Colorado. For centuries the Colorado had run its 1,400-mile race to the sea unchecked, and each spring melted snow would swell the river until it flooded the lowlands. Farms were wiped out, with water standing over sprouted wheat, and the farms that did not wash out in the spring frequently blew away in the fall and winter, when the ''mighty'' Colorado vanished except for a trickle.

Disastrous floods in 1905, and again in 1907, which swept downriver in the Imperial Valley and southern California, added incentive to harness the river. It was a long, drawn-out project. But finally in 1928, Congress passed the Boulder Canyon Project Act, authorizing construction of Hoover Dam and the All-American Canal System. Hoover Dam, just minutes from downtown Las Vegas, was the key to downstream control and regulation: since it was completed in 1935, there has not been a flood or drought on lands watered by the Colorado River.

If this region had only the Colorado River and Hoover Dam, it would still be rich. The dam harnesses the river for both irrigation and energy. When the government authorized the building of what was then called Boulder Dam, they also began construction of a town for the workers. Two million dollars built the town of Boulder City, a look-alike government housing project that the government rented back to the workers. Years of construction took place at the dam before high voltage lines were built up the canyons, and giant steel-legged towers radiated from Boulder City as electricity was fed as far away as southern California.

A visitor to the dam shortly after it was completed recounts, ''I remember set in the pavement on the Nevada end was a bronze diagram of the stars and planets the way they were arranged at the time the dam was dedicated. Seeing the dam firsthand, you could understand why the universe was on the plaque. The dam was just immense. I crossed over to the Arizona side on a road along the top of the dam, and looking down, the powerhouses appeared as something from a toy village. They did not look real. I will have to say that the immenseness of the man-made dam affected me like no other in my life, and I'm better than 70 years old.''

On February 1, 1935, two years ahead of schedule, the water of the Colorado was first trapped. The world's largest man-made object, which contained three and one-quarter-million cubic yards of concrete, began backing up water to fill Lake Mead. As the water flooded the arid canyon country, it took with it the sites of several towns and settlements. One town above Black Canyon rapids was the Mormon settlement of St. Thomas. Houses were still standing, buckboards parked in the lanes, when Lake Mead began to fill. But like Atlantis rising, in the years of low water, the mud-caked shell of St. Thomas rises from Lake Mead.

Lake Mead reflects the mood of the desert that surrounds it. A setting sun of brilliant colors fades to soft pastels, and islands jutting above the surface break a perfect reflection with their shadows. The lake can brood coldly in the winter months as flocks of ducks and geese rise from protected inlets to fly further south. In spring the water warms: every form of wildlife stirs, and before long happy boaters and skiers are cutting the surface as the sunlight paints rainbows through the spray. During the hot months, Lake Mead is a cool haven.

Besides the obvious value for flood control and recreation potential, Lake Mead and Hoover Dam generate 1.3 million kilowatts at capacity from the 17 generators. And the water has made the farmland bloom. Behind the dam is stored nearly two years of average Colorado River flow. The water is released in a regulated year-round flow to farms, homes and factories. It irrigates three-quarters of a million acres of land in this country and nearly a million in Mexico, some of the finest cropland in the world. The valleys and low mesas in the warm desert climate, once they have water, will produce winter fruits and vegetables that find their way to America's dinner tables during any season of the year.

Since Lake Mead was created, it has become one of the Southwest's most popular recreation areas. The twelve-month season attracts more than five-million visitors a year to enjoy swimming, boating, water skiing, and, of course, fishing. Lake Mead has the reputation for a wide array of good-eating fish. There are large-mouth bass, bluegill, black crappie, trout and channel catfish. With more than 500 miles of unspoiled shoreline, and water so still and clear it looks like a mirror, Lake Mead

The Landmark from the Desert Inn golf course

18

The Caesar's Palace Fountain and Winged Victory statue

The desert in bloom, east of Las Vegas

20

Spring Mountain Ranch State Park
(Following pages) Flamingo and Dunes Hotels from the Dunes golf course

Shoshone Mountains and the Reese River

Cactus in bloom, Willow Beach

Toiyade Range from Big Smokey Valley

The Convention Center

Fremont Street at night

Golfing in Las Vegas

Boulder Dam

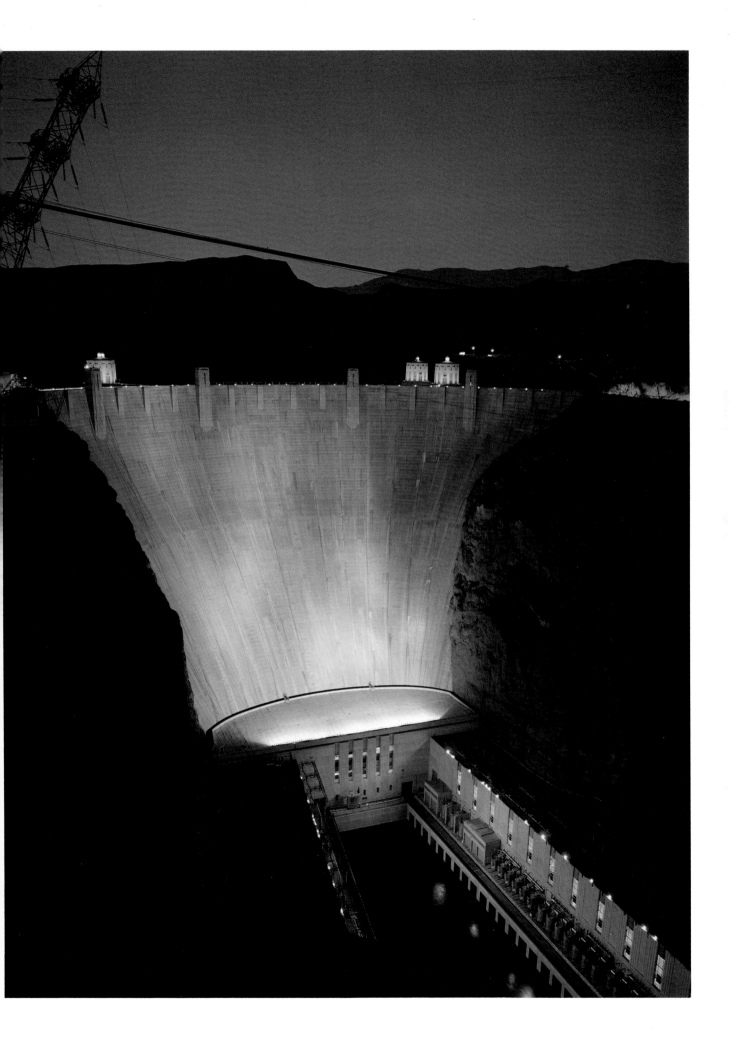

Valley of Fire State Park

Cathedral Gorge near Pioche

Las Vegas at evening from the roof of the Mint
(Following pages) Red Rock Canyon area

Caesar's Palace fountains and the Flamingo, from Caesar's Palace

Willow Beach Marina, Lake Mojave

University of Nevada, Las Vegas

Cactus garden, Lake Mead Recreation Area

The ghost town of Rhyolite

Lake Mead from Stewart's Point

The Landmark from the Desert Inn golf course

The Showboat
(Following page) Valley of Fire State Park

The Escarpment from Spring Mountain Ranch
(Preceding page) Desert from the Mt. Charleston area

The Calico Hills in the Red Rock Canyon area

50

"The Cabins," Valley of Fire State Park

The Casino swimming pool

Wildflowers and Lake Mead

Southern Nevada sunset
(Following pages) Valley of Fire State Park

Road to Cold Creek Camp, Mt. Charleston area

58

University of Nevada campus
(Following pages) Valley of Fire State Park

Las Vegas Strip from the top of the Dunes Hotel

Valley of Fire State Park

offers the best of the worlds of desert and water. The lake, sometimes described as "where the water laps the sage," is administered by the National Park Service.

But Lake Mead isn't all. Below the tailrace of Hoover Dam begins Lake Mojave. Its waters extend for 67 miles downstream to Davis Dam. The cold waters, coming from the depths of Lake Mead, provide for excellent trout fishing. And when those trout take the hook, they fight.

If you leave Las Vegas in the *other* direction—west—it's about a 40-minute drive to 12,000-foot Mt. Charleston. The setting is cool and refreshing, with pine-scented air, picnic grounds, and chances for long summer walks. The Spring Mountain Range, of which Charleston Peak is one, is a surprise to every visitor, rising sharply as they do from the desert floor. The cool mountain air is a delightful shock to the body, and the aspen oasis looks out of place after viewing yucca plants in the desert. Deer, chokecherries, and wild strawberries are everywhere. For wintertime skiing, Lee Canyon, with its 3,000-foot double chairlift, chalet and cocktail lounge, is gaining a wide and faithful following. Hunters in the varied terrain will find their prospects good for dove, quail, mule deer, elk, and mountain sheep.

From the top of Charleston Peak it is possible to look north toward Frenchman's Flat, where the Atomic Energy Commission has been detonating nuclear devices since January 27, 1951. In the 25 years that followed, there have been 306 announced nuclear detonations, all but 84 of these conducted underground. Of particular interest is the Sedan crater. Two days after Independence Day, 1962, the Sedan test was detonated. The 100-kiloton device, buried 635 feet underground, moved 12-million tons of material, and created a crater 320 feet deep and more than 1,250 feet across.

North of Las Vegas, on the upper arm of Lake Mead, is Valley of Fire State Park. Here can be found Indian petroglyphs, which date back 1,500 years. This region boasts a series of unusual rock formations: Elephant Rock, the Bee Hives, Mouse's Tank, and a natural basin that gathers and stores moisture. The blazing red sandstone makes it look as if the entire area was transported from some distant planet. Visitors interested in the past will enjoy viewing the artifacts of ancient Indian civilizations on display in Lost City Museum, located a few miles away in Overton.

If you have arrived in Las Vegas without a car, you'll find a number of ready-made bus tours which will carry you to near or distant destinations. A bus-and-boat tour of Lake Mead is popular, but other tours take visitors farther afield, for a look at the natural wonders of Zion National Park, Grand Canyon National Park, Bryce

Canyon in southern Utah, and Death Valley in California, all of which are closer to Las Vegas than one might expect. For a really unforgettable experience, the visitor should try Scenic Airline's tour of the Grand Canyon. The scenery is breathtaking, and for a closer look, the pilot will drop down between the sheer canyon walls!

For history buffs caught up in the romance of gold and gunbattles in the Old West, there is lots of adventure in the Las Vegas area. One such commercialized venture is Old Nevada, a duplicate wild west town about 30 miles from Las Vegas. Guests usually arrive aboard charter buses and find a Miner's Restaurant, a Dance Hall, an Ice Cream Parlor and an Old Time Saloon, where adults can pour their own drinks from the bottle. Daily features include convincing shoot-outs in the street, and realistic hangings. But there are other towns, ghost-like or nearly so, that remain ''unimproved,'' and the serious visitor will find them rewarding. The remains of Potosi, Sandy Valley, and Eldorado Canyon are all less than an hour's drive from downtown, accessible on paved or well-graded roads. And if exploring old towns seems interesting, add Searchlight and Goodsprings to your list. They are towns, still living, that experienced mineral booms near the turn of the century.

The best preserved ghost town in Nevada's southern sector is further afield, but still within a day's drive of Las Vegas. Rhyolite's feature attraction is a house constructed entirely from bottles. Quart beer bottles were laid horizontally with adobe for mortar; Victorian jigsaw frills were hung from the eaves of the gabled roof. The Bottle House is a sight the visitor won't want to miss.

For those with adventure in their hearts, there are still minerals waiting to be discovered. Gold or silver deposits could be hiding just below the surface in some off-the-road area. But before you start digging, check with local authorities. And be careful of old mining shafts.

A short afternoon could take a curious traveler to the sandstone ridges of Calico Hills. The soft, subtle pinks and tans of the hills are only 16 miles from the Las Vegas Strip. To get there, go west on West Charles Boulevard about 16 miles, and turn at Calico Basin. A broad meadow, carpeted with grass and dotted by cottonwood shade trees, makes a rendezvous point for hiking trails that radiate in all directions. The colors of the richly-hued hills offer a visual delight. Children soon discover the fun of rock scrambling.

Two miles past the Calico Basin turnoff, Red Rock Canyon Scenic Drive begins. Nine miles in is Willow Springs campground. But in spite of the name, no drinking water is available. It's a good idea to carry your own. On the faces of the sandstone cliffs, which crowd close to the road, are petroglyphs done by Paiute Indians. They made this canyon home for periods of time, and etched symbols and pictures on the sandstone walls.

The same drive out of Las Vegas can be modified to include Spring Mountain Ranch, as well. It is an interesting historic site, which is now run by the Nevada Division of State Parks. The 528-acre spread became a working cattle ranch in 1864. A long line of owners, including the late Howard Hughes, changed the working cattle ranch into a luxurious retreat. Today, at Spring Mountain Ranch, there is a meeting of the western cowboy and the vacationer and sightseer. Tours of the ranch-house are free. Not far from the headquarters area is an open meadow with picnic facilities. In the rugged sandstone bluffs that provide the backdrop, it is not uncommon to see a cowboy on his horse, slowly picking his way through the rock and sagebrush.

Local Color

Living on the land can be accomplished in several ways, and southern Nevada has seen most of them in the time that human beings have lived there. The first way is to harvest what is already there—the wildlife, plants for food and building materials, and so on. Another is to plant crops and harvest them, and where conditions allowed farmers to irrigate, that approach has been successful since the time of Anasazi. Where irrigation isn't possible, the best idea, usually, is to raise animals which can prosper on mesquite, range grass and sage brush, and make a living from the animals. And finally, if you can't make a living from what grows on the land or walks over it, you can always dig for the riches that lie underneath it. All of those things have happened at one time or another in southern Nevada. But the people who left the most vivid impression are the cowboys, the sheepherders, and the miners, who called this land home in the early days.

> "A cowboy in blue chaps climbs over the rail in Chute No. 1. Below him, like dynamite, waits a ton of Brahma bull. Pulling his rawhide glove down tight, the cowboy welds it to the rope, takes a deep seat and nods to the chute-man to 'open her up.'
>
> "Out in the arena, sunlight is filtering through dust as the clown moves to meet the bull. Dressed in bright red, the clown looks ridiculous in every way except for his feet: he wears soccer shoes for traction. The bull begins a quick turn back toward the clown, and the rider with the blue chaps gets twisted. His cowboy hat is suspended in mid-air and the rider, if his motion were stopped, would look like he had his thumb plugged in a light socket."

The rodeo is the heartbeat of the Old West. It is what the cowboy is about. A good horse or two, and a herd of cattle, is all a cowboy ever asks. And the rangeland surrounding Las Vegas produces some of the best cows and cowboys the West has ever seen.

The history of the cattle country began with the exploration by Spaniard Don Francisco Vasquez de Coronado, in the 1540s. He searched for the fabled, but illusory, Seven Cities of Gold. For food and barter he trailed a herd of cattle. No record remains to show if any of these animals survived to breed in present Nevada.

It is, in fact, impossible to tell the exact date cattle entered and remained in the area. But it is known that immigrants to California, from the 1840s onward, did bring livestock, and, undoubtedly, some got loose or strayed without being recovered. Some pioneer diaries give an insight into the number of cattle they brought, in what they called their "cow column." From Captain Sol Tetherow's journal of 1845 comes the notation that the train consisted of "66 wagons, 293 persons, 44 cattle drovers, 624 head loose cattle and 398 oxen."

With the immigrants came a division of land. At first, the pioneers were all headed for California, but in time they began to double back and stay in the Great Basin country. With property lines came fences. Cattle barons lost sections of open range. With smaller acreages available, new ranchers concentrated on improving the quality of the breeds.

For years the most popular breed had been Texas Longhorns, because they were so readily available. As other breeds reached Nevada, a cross-breed, a rugged wide-forager, was developed. When the steers were ready for market, they were trailed. For years the area was subject to California market prices, controlled by Miller and Lux. However, when the Union Stock Yards of Chicago opened and the railroad was completed in 1869, there was unlimited opportunity for area ranchers. They could raise the highest quality of cattle known, and have a market.

Cattlemen over the years have had to weather everything God and man have thrown in their direction—winters that kill up to 90% of the stock, theft, low prices for selling and high prices for shipping. The cattleman is a tough breed. He endures.

Every spring on Nevada ranches is branding time. The cows bellow and bawl, and the calves, from inside the holding pen, answer in return, as one by one they are herded down an alleyway. At the end, modern-day cowboys trap the calves in metal contraptions called "squeeze chutes" and brand every one. Each animal receives a vaccination: cattlemen around Las Vegas pride themselves on having cattle nearly free of disease.

The sheepherder should have a monument dedicated to him. He is the man who stays with his band and only gets to town once or twice a year. The Basques, in particular, were famous for their herding abilities and dedication: many a herder suffered frozen feet or lost fingers circling his flock in a blizzard. Without dedicated, hard-working sheepherders, the sheep industry on the open range would not exist. The Las Vegas area has a favorable climate for wintering sheep. Bands numbering into the thousands are driven as much as 400 miles to avail them of the moderate weather.

"It's a good life, she is," spoke a sheepherder. He sat on the step of his home: a wagon covered with an arch of tin, which from a distance, had appeared to be a soup can on wheels.

Inside, on the small woodburning stove, a stew was simmering and coffee was on. The sheepherder asked if I would like to stay for dinner. There were biscuits and fresh huckleberry jam that melted in my mouth. And after eating and talking around the fire, I unrolled a sleeping bag a ways away. When I awoke the herder was gone, and so were his sheep.

Yes sir, there ought to be a monument dedicated to sheepherders.

The advent of the automobile opened Great Basin mining. Prospectors could drive to likely spots, take a sample, and if the ore graded, they were in business. But mining began long before the automobile was invented.

One of the wildest early-day strikes was near the Colorado River in Eldorado Canyon. According to the story, ore was first recovered by a group of soldiers from Fort Mojave, who were camping in Eldorado Canyon in 1859. Some Las Vegas residents, who had experience at the Posoti mines, recognized that the ore contained both gold and silver. A group was formed, and a number of mining claims were staked.

A popular story of the Eldorado concerns a man by the name of John Nash, who tried to jump the Queen City claim and organize the Eldorado Company in 1874. Nash persuaded three bloodthirsty villians to join him in his efforts: Harrington, who had reportedly killed three men; Piette, an Indian renegade; and Jim Jones, a no-good character. Nash agreed to pay each man $500. He planned to cover his financial arrangement by having Piette kill his partners, after they had held the Queen City claim for the legal number of days.

Jim Jones was washing his face one morning when Piette slipped up behind him and fired what should have been a fatal shot. But instead of dying, Jones hurled the water-basin at Piette, then grabbed his gun and took a shot at him, finally escaping on foot. But Piette carried the day: he claimed *he* was the one who had been attacked; and he formed up a posse and started after Jim Jones.

It was no problem to follow Jones' bloody trail. The posse caught up with him at an old prospect hole, and shot him without benefit of a trial. John Nash's takeover of the Queen City mine was ultimately successful, and he saved himself the $500 that was Jim Jones' share.

The mining boom at Eldorado Canyon helped to open up the Colorado River for shipping. Eldorado had been determined years before to be the limit of navigation. However, when gold and silver were struck, the run upriver from Yuma became an everyday occurrence between May and September, when the river was high enough. Ship owners had a bonanza. But the good times ended on the Colorado when the steamboat *Searchlight* broke through a levee in 1906 and was lost. The *Searchlight* was the last steamer on the Colorado.

The town of Searchlight is up and away from the river. Until shipping ended in 1906, Searchlight was going strong. The town had its foundation in gold. In the early days one gold claim was traded for $1,500 cash, a team of mules, a buckboard and a double-barreled shotgun. Another claim that paid off for $150,000 was originally sold for a pint of whiskey. Over six million dollars worth of gold, and one lump of turquoise, which weighed 320 carats, came out of the district. While mining went on, Searchlight boasted as many as 38 saloons.

The hills around Searchlight, old-timers will tell you, are haunted: the result of a burro fight, which was the main attraction in town on Independence Day, 1902. As the story goes, talk started casually enough with miners swapping stories about the meanness of their animals. But the way things ended up, two noted Jacks, Thunder and Hornet, were nominated by the mining camps to fight it out for the title of Meanest Burro in Nevada. By the day of the fight, several thousand dollars had been wagered on the outcome. Thunder and Hornet started to fight as soon as they were turned loose. A cloud of dust rose up to conceal the battle, until finally, late in the day, Thunder broke out of the dust cloud and headed full-tilt for the soothing waters of the Colorado, never to return. Even today, old-timers will tell you, if you're down between Searchlight and Cottonwood Cove on the river, the hooves of the defeated mule can be heard—as Thunder comes rolling over the hill.

Photo Credits

Color Separations
by
Universal Color Corporation
Beaverton, Oregon/San Diego, California

Beautiful America Publishing Company

The nation's foremost publisher of quality color photography

Current Books

Alaska
Arizona
Boston
British Columbia
California
California Vol. II
California Coast
California Desert
California Missions
California Mountains
Chicago
Colorado
Dallas
Delaware
Denver
Florida
Georgia
Hawaii
Idaho
Illinois
Indiana
Kentucky
Las Vegas
Los Angeles, 200 Years

Maryland
Massachusetts
Michigan
Michigan Vol. II
Minnesota
Missouri
Montana
Montana Vol. II
Monterey Peninsula
Mormon
Mt. Hood (Oregon)
Nevada
New Jersey
New Mexico
New York
New York City
Northern California
Northern California Vol. II
North Carolina
North Idaho
Ohio
Oklahoma
Orange County
Oregon

Oregon Vol. II
Oregon Coast
Oregon Country
Pacific Coast
Pennsylvania
Pittsburgh
San Diego
San Francisco
San Juan Islands
Seattle
Tennessee
Texas
Utah
Utah Country
Vancouver U.S.A.
Vermont
Virginia
Volcano Mt. St. Helens
Washington
Washington Vol. II
Washington, D.C.
Wisconsin
Wyoming
Yosemite National Park

Forthcoming Books

Alabama
Arkansas
Baltimore
Connecticut
Detroit
The Great Lakes
Houston
Kansas

Kauai
Maine
Maui
Mississippi
New England
New Hampshire
North Dakota

Oahu
Phoenix
Rhode Island
Rocky Mountains
South Carolina
South Dakota
West Virginia

Large Format, Hardbound Books

Beautiful America
Beauty of California
Beauty of Oregon

Beauty of Washington
Glory of Nature's Form
Volcanoes of the West

Lewis & Clark Country
Western Impressions